Field Music

▲

Seth Jani

FUTURECYCLE PRESS
www.futurecycle.org

Cover artwork by Emerson Antcliff; author photo by Rebekah Gehrke; cover and interior design by Diane Kistner; Adobe Garamond Pro text and Macondo titling

Library of Congress Control Number: 2022944647

Published by FutureCycle Press
Athens, Georgia, USA

ISBN 978-1-952593-36-9

Contents

Beginner's Mind....5
Selva Antica....6
Field Music....7
Garden Wall....8
Sentinel....9
Alchemy....10
Resident Forces....11
Hurricane Lamp....12
New Moon....13
The Balloons....14
Odonata....15
Bread....16
Bare Hymn....17
The Beekeeper....18
Credo....19
The Blue Hour....20
Western Sky....21
After Dark....22
Aion....23
Border Stones....24
Honey Psalm....25
Hatchery Brook....26
Telemachus Creek....27
Paper Lanterns....28
The Blackout....29
September....30
Storm Cellar....31
Cemetery Hill....32
Waning....33
Coming and Going....34
Navigators....35
Buried Colors....36
Winter Comes to the Coffee-Colored Earth....37
Stone Table....38
Birdwatching....39
The Heron....40
The Wood Grouse....41
Courses....42

Barn Song....43
The Blaze....44
These Ruins....45
Midwinter....46
Maps....47
The Valley....48
Master of Tides....49
The Hunt....50
Poetry....51
Permission to Land....52
Curriculum Vitae....53
For the Wayfarers....54

Beginner's Mind

Again it comes, like a stone
caught in the wheel, like a fire
leveling the valley, overturning
a life's perceptions.
No monasteries remain,
no stacks of irreplaceable content.
The student learns she must begin
with only a few leaves left to study.
They are first pages, turning over
and over in the empty wind.

Selva Antica

He falsified nothing.
The forest was there
percolating life
from the deep waters,
unknotting his mind
in the complexity of groves,
the reason-defying foliage.
When he finally lost
the logician's zest
for making doors,
he found the light
protracted everywhere.
The deer roamed quietly
while his tensions faltered.
He felt their softness
nuzzle against his body.
And even the rocks taught him
a hard, industrious joy.

Field Music

The dead are playing their pianos
in the circus ring of trees.

It's midnight, and the moth burns,
then starts out on new, dark wings.

It's best here to drink from the river
where the music leads.

Its water is a soft breathing emerald,
a fire under glass.

It might be the home of all our molecules,
the reason why something reaches out

when the rain arrives.
Its gravity is secret and colossal,

bends us into a chorus,
refracted voices emerging

from every porous joint,
every wild fissure.

It causes even the small darkness
of our pupils to shine like winter stones.

Garden Wall

On the stone, the frost-hemmed
fingerprint of the questioner
keeps shining.
After all his obsession
with mortal things,
his beautiful confusions,
there is only this pattern of DNA
holding out a little longer
before the sunlight hits the wall.

Sentinel

The astral double drifts
between this world and
the next, which may or
may not exist,
though we lean towards belief
when, sometimes, in the perfect
angles of the rain, we glimpse
the sumac catching fire,
its inner body ghosting
the retina, lifting its mask
of sodden foliage to reveal
a fierce sentry. The heart, too,
is like this: a shriveled organ
that bursts into hosannas
or cooks up mirages from
the feeding light of desire.
We are pinned to a mystery,
mitochondrial, and big as an
extinct language.

Alchemy

The forest is everywhere
like someone's lung blown
inside out by a largening wind,
a red corolla emerging from
the mouth,
becoming a place for bees,
the dangerous work
of transmuting honey out of air.
We circulate in that stream,
our whole lives beautifully
stitched and heathered
by the expelled breath
of trees.

Resident Forces

Even our cemeteries
are stripped clean of ghosts—
the linoleum light washing off
the thousand-headed stones
and leaving a single cairn.
But the earth is really a simulcast
of multiple frequencies:
blue camenae and the green inhabitants
in the green trees.
Not to mention the known invisibilities:
tardigrades wedged between dewdrops,
the magic of atoms
conjuring touch in the lovers' hands.

Hurricane Lamp

We protect it from the wind,
which of all things is made
for scattering, for the diffusion of light.
It might be anger, sorrow,
the pull of flesh and longing,
or maybe just some blind obsessive tic.
Either way, we keep the flame
calmly lit and wait for the natural bend
towards darkness, the karmic snuffing.
We do not want to waste
a single cause for radiance.
There is precious little fuel.

New Moon

No theories arise when the wind
hits the centerpiece and sends it
toppling to the floor.
Things will be as they are,
and the fallen candles
form a heap of ashes for the
scavenging mouse to find.
She will mend her darkness
whether we catch her or not.
And even when our civilization has ended,
geologically or in a fluke
of our own devising, this same moon
that flares through midnight's window
will continue its age-old provocation,
becoming the place where another
generation of sleepwalkers
send their light-rigged prayers.

The Balloons

Beautiful patchwork filling
the morning sky
and some old eruption
dotting the landscape
with gem and basalt.
No worry if we are
better or worse than others.
Knee-deep in dragon scales,
we wander the petrified forest,
collecting geodes in our hearts.
We should treat the world
as if it were made of diamonds:
everything quietly reflected
and, afterward, just silver glass.
A plane passes over,
and we don't fear the passing.
A field reveals hidden bodies,
and we don't fear the eventual process.
The wicker baskets lift
from the canyon floor,
carrying their happy passengers
nowhere terribly special.

Odonata

I moved the prow,
which was treading light
more than seawater, and turned it towards
the crux of new beginnings,
those bright solstices.
No one had a compass,
but the stars were enough
and the balanced needles of the heart
and that other magnetic force
we cannot name.
We are never really lost.
We find a circle on the map
at the place where a dragonfly
set down.
Its feet were made of fire,
and the magical prints
resemble an island.
Odonata, we call it,
and there is no reason to fear
as long as those rainbow-colored
wings exist.
O circumneural waters!
Cascading fauna!
We have been chasing
all night your green locus.
This beautiful, multilayered world
is all we need.

Bread

I opened doors because I was obsessed
with the light beyond them,
though no one else shared my happiness
when dragonflies filled the hall.
The windows were shut and the book
of fables burned for kindling.
I planted small moons in the sky outside,
preparing for famine,
for the hunger to be born.
It didn't matter that the streets
were covered in darkness
or that the people only believed
in nameable weathers.
Flowers fell and ignited the pavement.
June came and went
with its sacraments of rain.

Bare Hymn

I rise up, Saint Francis,
into the simplicity of night,
the field and industry
of joy.
We have been burdened
for so long,
and the animals come
with such lightness,
such timidity in their steps.
See that hand reaching out
and grazing the world of innocence?
What does it bring back?
In the place where the mower doesn't go
there is a hard presence.
The white stones stand by it.
All it takes is a close eye,
an ear tilted to the wind.
All it takes is absolute stillness.
The water in the garden
fills with reflections.
A small wing nests
inside the light.

The Beekeeper

Enter yellow light
through the tunnels
in the heart
where the vital energies
keep us breathing,
keep us happily here
on this sunny escalade
towards the golden hive.
I dream of honey so often
that I feel my blood stick
in the thin pass of arteries.
All my days have been spent
on the tops of ladders
searching for the sweet spot
between the earth and sky.
The bees guard that middle kingdom,
alternately fierce and beautiful,
and when their weltering stings
send me running across the fields,
it's like a sentence
condemning me to tend
the garden of my life.

Credo

I am simplifying my philosophies:
Life, my friends, is a swirling dream-fuck.

We are souls confused and incognito.

We are small factories churning out
muddled signs of radiance.

We are flickers in some god's drug-hammered haze.

Or maybe we are tiny, irrelevant reeds
catching the wind, emptily and with joy,

in a moon-dark meadow the size of love.

The Blue Hour

Dusk comes to me
with all her baskets,
singing.
I follow her through
the stages of night,
the degrees of darkness.
Awareness at this hour
has a purple tinge,
and all our obsessions
are exhausted.
The breeze undoes
the stolid points,
opening pools
where a feather sets down
and doesn't vanish.
It will drift there forever,
like the light that fell long ago
across the shale roof
and still illuminates
the inner face of memory.
I come out of the forest
and almost believe there
really is a ghost inside my body.
It's just a name, though,
tied to a persistent illusion
formed in the crucible
of the moon and trees.

Western Sky

Here, in this part of the universe,
everything has happened.
But over there, it's only yesterday,
and the beautiful pause of death
is still waiting for the notes to settle,
for the music to subside.
I have been in an ocean
that defies everything we believe in.
I have spent a day watching forms
arise and disappear.
The wind erases all our names,
and we hear someone blow
on the slender grass blades.
The whole field fills
with luminous sound.
I think just beyond the
radius of water, the nocturnal pools,
a small bird is engulfed in light.
You might say imagination
gets the better of me, but I believe
this radiance is commonplace.
The ordinary miracle of the moon
is an insomniac torching the western sky.
Despite our reservations,
these glass-blown evenings pop
with ancient stars.

After Dark

Horticulturists sing their sun-
colored plants to sleep,
and the night itself responds
by turning their bodies white,
revealing another aspect, another
season, another side to things.
All through the garden,
the statues suddenly respire.
It might be a trick from the moon's
library of incantations,
or maybe it's just the old logician
setting down his disbelief.
Either way, the magic is real.
The dragonflies shine
like painted glass.

Aion

He plays his instrument
in the beginning phases
of night.
It's half wind,
half percussing moth,
and in between
the stillness of pines.
Whenever he pauses,
a green minute
fills the midnight clock.
He creates a new kind
of time, nothing that resembles
the petty calculations
on the wrists of quiet sleepers.
Only the insects understand it,
the night birds, the equatorial grasses.
Only the heart with its
sundered latitudes,
its light-measuring stones.

Border Stones

Even death is just a concept
we put on the bare facts of things.
Alluvium and *sunlight*—
names for the annealing world,
the dough that turns into bread.
I forfeit opinions because
I want the startled wings without
the assumption of the bird.
In the forest, I'm simply dazzled.
My heart may hurt, but I won't be caught
in its titular magic.
I'm a green ache in a green wood.
There's a little wind over there,
a pool of black water,
someone getting lost
in the high grasses.
The weight we carry is made up
mostly of imagination
and a couple pieces of the past.

Honey Psalm

Out to my hand
the limitless gold
is pouring and buzzing,
arriving through the early
August light
like a séance of bees.
Contrary to belief,
we are haunted
by gem-like beings
dispensing the music
of blessings.
The only ghosts
are the good ghosts
of the wind and rivers,
the bright shadows
of the other world
more solid than ourselves.
I step off the painted ladder
and into the summer air.
The pollen builds around me
the shape of the faithful.

Hatchery Brook

You watch the clouds arise
and thin into nothing.
Just like our own lives
undoing their knots
into empty space.
You were no one before
the beautiful convergence
gave you your name.
And now, all day, the landscape
belongs to your wandering.
It's a mistake to believe
we are only bits of dreaming matter.
The snowcaps return, year after year,
and they become something the same
but different.
We, too, grow out of ourselves
like a secret or seed.
We build our house
and, in the openness that follows,
we build it again.
The clear sky seems familiar.
The loons set down
and startle us awake.

Telemachus Creek

From every fault line of darkness,
a blue dragonfly skirts
the glistening stone.

This is the grace of August
coming to haunt us,
to fill the paltry day.

I cup my hands
and they fill with water.
I waltz in the descending night.

Overhead, a daylit moon
unsettles the heart,
dislodges the comfortable chains,

and the conflagrant self
steps out of the body,
solitary and luminous,

like that single bright godetia
on the summer hill.

Paper Lanterns

The self was invented
after it was discovered
that rocks plummet back to earth
when tossed towards the sky
and that all laws are the same
whether inside or out.
But this is assuming
that the self should be like a stone
and not a bird or flower,
a petal-light charm
drifting casually through morning.
This is assuming that the person
who rises in sleep
towards the midnight clouds
is an illusion
and that, in our moments of grace
when happiness breaks the pattern
of our anger, we are not experiencing
the wilder breath of truth
but simply a lapse in nature.
The self, then, is a clear bag
we filled with sand.
We've been carrying the weight for so long,
we forget it can be emptied,
that it can just as easily be filled
with wind and light,
ascending into the darkness
like a paper lantern
released over the dreaming lake.

The Blackout

I built a house and layered it
with everything I could gather
from the fringes of the wood:
blackberry, hawthorn, skulls the size of roses.
I thought I could protect my body
with the body of the world.
When winter came, nothing flourished.
Even my books lost their pages.
I thought I was waiting
for the blackout to occur.
Fixated on annihilation,
I almost didn't notice
that I became the winter grasses,
that the stream simply bent
around the corner,
that the forest exchanged its atoms
for another, identical place.

September

What happens is you find
something strange and ancient
in the bottom of your heart.
You're not sure what it is,
but your life suddenly changes
and the foundation stones start to sing.
Has there been music all this time
right in the center?
An undercurrent of grace
lighting the depths?
The moon arches out of nowhere
and bears the estranged mind home.
Someone sets down their grudges
for a final time.
A star crashes into the valley
carrying the fossil of a god.

Storm Cellar

This is one of the paradises
that we get to
by opening the blue-flaked door
and entering the earth.
By putting everything on hold
and saying *I love you,*
even as the battering rams
blow through our houses
and the malevolent rain
drills into the floor,
leaving us to stumble
into a second darkness
where the white flowers
are stark as serpents
and the roots of grace
are nearer to our feet.

Cemetery Hill

At sixteen I got drunk
in the cemetery down the road
and followed my desolate shadow
past the white flowers
into the surrounding woods.
I remember imagining my friends
caught by rain and six feet under,
each one of them growing out of their lives
into the dead-end dark,
the green light of spirits mostly imagined.
Now I am looking back and once again
comfortably lost, and I am counting the actual dead
on both my hands.
I am listening for the sacrament
the old New England wind
performs among the headstones,
its mouth full of names and ashes,
its luminous face turned towards mine.

Waning

The moon is a young ruin
still finding its way
through the trees.
I count my blessings:
that I am not a fallen thing,
that I know nothing of collapse
or resurrection,
that I can walk
into the driving wind
and it scarcely notices
my nominal life.
We spend our days wanting
to be greater than we are.
We suffer our little deaths
and think they are all that matter.
Take me to the field
where the heart shines
and the body blossoms.
Teach me to bear
my splinter of the light.

Coming and Going

All day, answers are falling
from the wind-napped petals
onto the starch-colored stone.
We can stop the masquerade right here
in the instant of summer's transition,
in the moment the page blows over
revealing sigils of whitened moss.
We were wrong to believe
we were ever someone.
Seasons and millennia equally span
the space between us.
It doesn't matter.
We wake when we wake
and may never know
the number of our wakings.
The pear tree stoops
its perfect umber into the yard
for the umpteenth time,
and no one ever mentions
the generations of fruit
on the valley floor.

Navigators

The spyglass opens over
the backward-treading sea
where the shipwrecked travel
in reverse, entering the kingdom
on a boat of silver glass.
Their journey is just beginning,
the coral washed from their bodies
and a small charm of navigation
hidden in their pockets.
They are pieces of a star that fell
like insect wings on the almost-
drafted map—the one that shows
a continent to be discovered,
a red dragon at the very center.
Those flame-dark hills are only
part of the imaginarium—
just like the moon, stunning
the subtropic eye with its
dazzling road.

Buried Colors

There's a blue in the heart
that resembles a parade of night birds
over the Atlantic,
that recalls the dark shapes
in the towers of Prague.
It's still as the mirroring waters,
as the radiant hush of thoughts.
After the trapped senses precipitate
like rain, you step out
into the dimming light.
The fireflies surround you,
and the lock-and-key of disbelief
breaks open.
Poetry and silence are two crystal eyes
in the body of awakening.
They're the reason why we alternately pray
and watch the blowing leaves.

Winter Comes to the Coffee-Colored Earth

The last bit of music drips down
from the summer pines.
No chimes left here, just dry wind
scouring the nooks of darkness,
lifting the luminous hackles
on the blackbird's neck.
The old town sinks
under the enchanted snow
that falls from the metallurgic clouds
with their divine and empty centers.
Past the sawmill, the eyes of strangers
call me back from the familiar road.
The ancient cisterns fill with water.
The sunflowers crack open
their rattled heads of light.

Stone Table

A fool in my own life,
the heart will flower
whether I believe in ghosts or reason,
whether I touch the dark-handed sea
or lean into the wind
with my fearful stones.
Empty or full, what I get is:
the sunlight on its spacious journey,
the fraught shadows, nearly golden,
the bread shared between friends,
the feast of gratitude
renewing over and over
our ancient bond.

Birdwatching

From the body of the stone
I am searching for the yellow wing
that haunts the sky,
the glimmer and incandescence
that sparks on the dark pool
of the pupil as if a galaxy were
exploding from inside.
We have many names
for the mysterious flash
that rattles our lives
from their dull cages
but no facts,
no designations beyond
the deep codes of fable.
When the music falls
from the twin-blooming trees,
it's like water stirring in a place
that's been so still for years
even the dead listen,
raising their flayed heads
from the cold echo chambers
in the mire's dusky caves.

The Heron

It arises from the edge of the lake,
no different than a dream
glass-blown by the breath of sleep.
It lingers a while, then turns
as if to face an empty wall.
Like Bodhidharma, it does not
fear the faceless or absolute.
It does not fear the morning wind.
It stands and passes through
the long stalks of light.
It becomes the mist.

The Wood Grouse

I can't dive
into the gold of flowers
without hearing
the petals
hit the earth.

It's autumn,
and I'm learning to process
the radial trees
in their decay,
the final egg
of the northern forest
with all its blue-green energy
pouring out of it.

We can collect the light
in our minds like sieves.
Who knows what diamonds
will be found there?
Snail shells? Remnant shards?
The potter's art?

If this is death
relaxing forms
so they can breathe,
then count my body happy.

The air nearly glitters
on its way to and from
my heart.

Courses

Maybe the sickness came
to make me tender,
to equalize a heart enchanted
by its own aloofness.
Among the river stones,
the sun was no longer
a streak of gold,
a resplendent eye.
It was a hard light,
and I hurt among familiar things.
The only solution was to sit inside
the pattern and be okay. Whether they
were my birds or not, beautiful wings
kept rushing by.

Barn Song

I'm not sure I could ever come
to the valley or the grave
without first touching
the green, acquitting light,
the dark shine of summer.
It's in my bones, thatched
out of sorrow, out of dawn break,
out of too many winters
taken to the chin.
It's in my heart, too,
which just last evening
was a red bird calling
from the conflagration,
from the burning house
my father set ablaze,
singing *mercy, mercy,*
there's no wind.

The Blaze

I built my temple in the mind
where the biologists claim
dead matter, bits of vanished tissue,
evolution's failed lot.
In-breath, out-breath,
and the reception changes.
I become myself
despite the verdict of obsoletion,
of mechanical absolutes.
The spirit is not lodged
here or there. It can be missed
but not dissected.
There's no getting out of the world,
even in death.
You vanish almost completely
but arise again.
It takes a little rain
falling in other centuries,
a roll of the die.
That troubled spot you can't move past
is where you built something holy once before.
You don't remember, but the fire was dear to you.
It helped you love your losses.
It taught you to rebuild.

These Ruins

My sorrow is ordinary,
and I lay it out beneath the trees
for the bone-picking birds to follow,
for the sun to open its seedpods of light
and drop onto.
I send it downriver
tied to a heart-shaped boat
where it will easily break
in the hands of children
and the someday-fire will calcify,
becoming just another stone house
abandoned to the wind.

Midwinter

This far out there is
Flame and Distance,
there is someone coming
to and from the dark,
there is transformation
turning the green wind
into a prism of light.
Winter moves in
as a beautiful addendum,
a black scrawl across the earth.
We enter its radius
like begrudging ghosts
called back to their hauntings,
to the place where memory etched
its crucial wound.
Afterward, the ink spills
and we call it *nighttime,*
we call it *shipwreck in the hearts of trees.*
We look out over the purple ruins,
that great edge we fear.

Maps

A traveler over the continents
of earth and sky found himself
in a place marked on the map
by a mythic bird.
It wasn't supposed to exist,
but there it was shining
like a basilisk's tooth,
rising from the seafloor
and piercing the aorta of clouds.
When the red rain fell,
he found the stone covered in bright manna,
and all the animals he encountered
in the dreams of childhood
came lumbering from the shadows,
lapping the astonishment from his hands.
Over the fading architecture
of the ancient city,
a beautiful moon cast
a translucent light.
Everything turned to glass.
One could see the inner life
of cicadas and the dark heartwood
of summer trees. One could hear
the vows of the universe, luminous and
salvific, hidden in the caliginous purr
of evening wind.

The Valley

A plane crashes and appears
as a red diamond
sinking into the sea.
A life crashes, too,
flaming like a star
on a molten night.
We think it's the end of everything
but, really, it's just the beginning.
Happiness falls into sorrow;
sorrow rises into air.
Desire cuts its obsessive cord
and becomes a cloud.
Life and death paint
their twin murals on either side
of the marble hall.
We walk through the valley,
examining textures and angles,
waiting out delusion
until our hearts are patient
and exact.

Master of Tides

This night, the monuments of grace
outweigh the monuments of desire.
They shine in the moonlight
like twisted trees.
They fill with birds
and spread out over the horizon
a tapestry of song.
Your sorrow leaves you.
Your fear wilts into a flower.
Certainty pours its milk
over all the doubts
in the ten-thousand corners
of your heart.
The ghosts grow silent
and take on the bodies of stones.
They mark the landscape,
become a path.
It's not your power
that makes this happen.
It's not your cleverness,
your serenity or rage.
It's just this: the light
filling the branches,
the moon sailing overhead.

The Hunt

I would step out of my body
to dream I was concurrent
with the wind and light
or the painted stones
tossed over the embankment
into the hearts of rivers.
I would grow more frail
than the gossamer knot
holding me together
in a spliff of consciousness.
We suffer in the digestive zone
of higher orders.
We believe ourselves angelic
in the drunk and ramshackle night.
The benevolent seeds cause flowers
to erupt from the dark non grata.
They are not our doing, though they allow
the spectacle of beauty to cross
our eyes.
I was a child wholly in love
with a green world I didn't know
would perish. I've never wept
in the open ruins.
It's a privilege to be alive,
even in the blaze of scarcity,
even in the desperate hunt
for transformation and bread.

Poetry

Poetry was my first door to the spirit.
Not religion. Not music. Not even the moon
with its silver immolations.
Though I never believed in magic
or even the accidental spark of grace,
you couldn't say I wasn't blessed
or the recipient of blessings.
I traced my lineage back
through the library's darkened shelves
until I became pure image.
My heart forfeited its horses
for the measureless road.
I found twilight in my pockets.
I waited for the drip of beatitude
on my fevered tongue.

Permission to Land

Hold out your hands
and touch the edges of the night
as it comes down over the Cascades.
Repeat to yourself the one thing
you know to be true,
whatever it may be.
When the wings catch your breath
on their vast migration,
let yourself be stunned for days.
The happiness of the world
depends on each one of us
sharing our sense of awe.
Don't let it be diminished.
Let it hold you
through the dull hours
and the nominal flares of darkness.
Let it be a wind that raises your hair
even in the greyness of routine.
Let it rest inside your memory
like your mother's cooking
or your father's long smile
into the fading light.

Curriculum Vitae

I was never a warrior,
a collector of bombs,
a fanatical convert to rage.
I never dreamed of exploding waters,
incinerated bones.
I had no love of country,
the dark god of borders.
What I loved instead
was the orchard of wild grass
that opens in the heart like doors;
the creek that becomes a shining temple,
a place of glass that takes our seeing
into its delicate, cold hands.
What I loved was the equation
of being in everyone,
their peculiar happening,
their idiosyncratic selves
beautiful as small animals.
I was not a warrior,
but I was fierce in my joy
for this world,
in my predilection for rain,
my finesse for deserts and forests.
When I say I was in love,
I mean with the green multitudes,
the wonderful little ghosts
of the trees and rivers.

For the Wayfarers

A poem is just a poem.
You want it to feed the hungry,
light candles for the dead,
capture the glistening wing
as it turns over the water.
At best, it promises satiation,
memorializes, turns blue.
We find many inadequate things
in our search for perfect love.
The bicycle breaks. The road goes on.
We settle at a way station and call it home.
Whoever you are, it is getting late.
The light fills the golden wheel
of clouds. The hand, once luminous,
grows dark. Footsteps turn into flowers
on the distant hill.

Acknowledgments

The author gratefully acknowledges the journals in which many of these poems first appeared:

Adelaide Literary Magazine: “Bare Hymn”
Amaryllis: “These Ruins”
The American Poetry Journal: “Sentinel”
Amethyst Review: “Master of Tides,” “Poetry,” ”The Blaze,” “Western Sky”
Blue Unicorn: “Hurricane Lamp”
Chiron Review: “Aion,” “Stone Table”
Common Ground Review: “Curriculum Vitae”
The Comstock Review: “Waning”
CP Quarterly: “For the Wayfarers”
Déraciné: “Midwinter”
Dunes Review: “Barn Song,” “Bread”
Eclectica Magazine: “After Dark”
Feral: A Journal of Poetry and Art: “Maps”
Good Works Review: “Coming and Going,” “The Balloons”
Hedge Apple: “Storm Cellar,” “Telemachus Creek”
The Metaworker: “The Hunt”
Nine Muses Poetry: “New Moon”
Nixes Mate Review: “Alchemy”
Occulum: “*Odonata*”
Oracle Fine Arts Review: “Field Music”
Petrichor: “*Selva Antica*”
Phantom Drift: “Navigators”
Psaltery & Lyre: “The Blue Hour”
Quail Bell Magazine: “Credo”
River and South Review: “The Wood Grouse”
Selcouth Station: “Buried Colors”
Serving House Journal: “Garden Wall”
Sheila-Na-Gig (online Summer Contest Winner): “Birdwatching,” “The Valley”
Subprimal Poetry Art: “Beginner’s Mind”
Sweet Tree Review: “Courses”
Sylvia: “Honey Psalm”
Visitant: “Border Stones,” “Paper Lanterns”
Whale Road Review: “Resident Forces”

About FutureCycle Press

FutureCycle Press is dedicated to publishing lasting English-language poetry in both print-on-demand and Kindle formats. Founded in 2007 by long-time independent editor/publishers and partners Diane Kistner and Robert S. King, the press was incorporated as a nonprofit in 2012. A number of our editors are distinguished poets and writers in their own right, and we have been actively involved in the small press movement going back to the early seventies.

Each year, we award the FutureCycle Poetry Book Prize and honorarium for the best original full-length volume of poetry we published that year. Introduced in 2013, proceeds from our Good Works projects are donated to charity. Our Selected Poems series highlights contemporary poets with a substantial body of work to their credit; with this series we strive to resurrect work that has had limited distribution and is now out of print.

We are dedicated to giving all of the authors we publish the care their work deserves, offering a catalog of the most diverse and distinguished work possible, and paying forward any earnings to fund more great books. All of our books are kept "alive" and available unless and until an author requests a title be taken out of print.

We've learned a few things about independent publishing over the years. We've also evolved a unique and resilient publishing model that allows us to focus mainly on vetting and preserving for posterity poetry collections of exceptional quality without becoming overwhelmed with bookkeeping and mailing, fundraising activities, or taxing editorial and production "bubbles." To find out more, come see us at futurecycle.org.

The FutureCycle Poetry Book Prize

All original, full-length poetry books published by FutureCycle Press in a given calendar year are considered for the annual FutureCycle Poetry Book Prize. This allows us to consider each submission on its own merits, outside of the context of a traditional contest. Too, the judges see the finished book, which will have benefitted from the beautiful book design and strong editorial gloss we are famous for.

The book ranked the best in judging is announced as the prize-winner in January of the subsequent year. There is no fixed monetary award; instead, the winning poet receives an honorarium of 20% of the total net royalties from all poetry books and chapbooks the press sold online in the year the winning book was published. The winner is also accorded the honor of being on the panel of judges for the next year's competition; all judges receive copies of the contending books to keep for their personal library.

www.ingramcontent.com/pod-product-compliance
Lightning Source LLC
LaVergne TN
LVHW020049110826
845155LV00029B/705